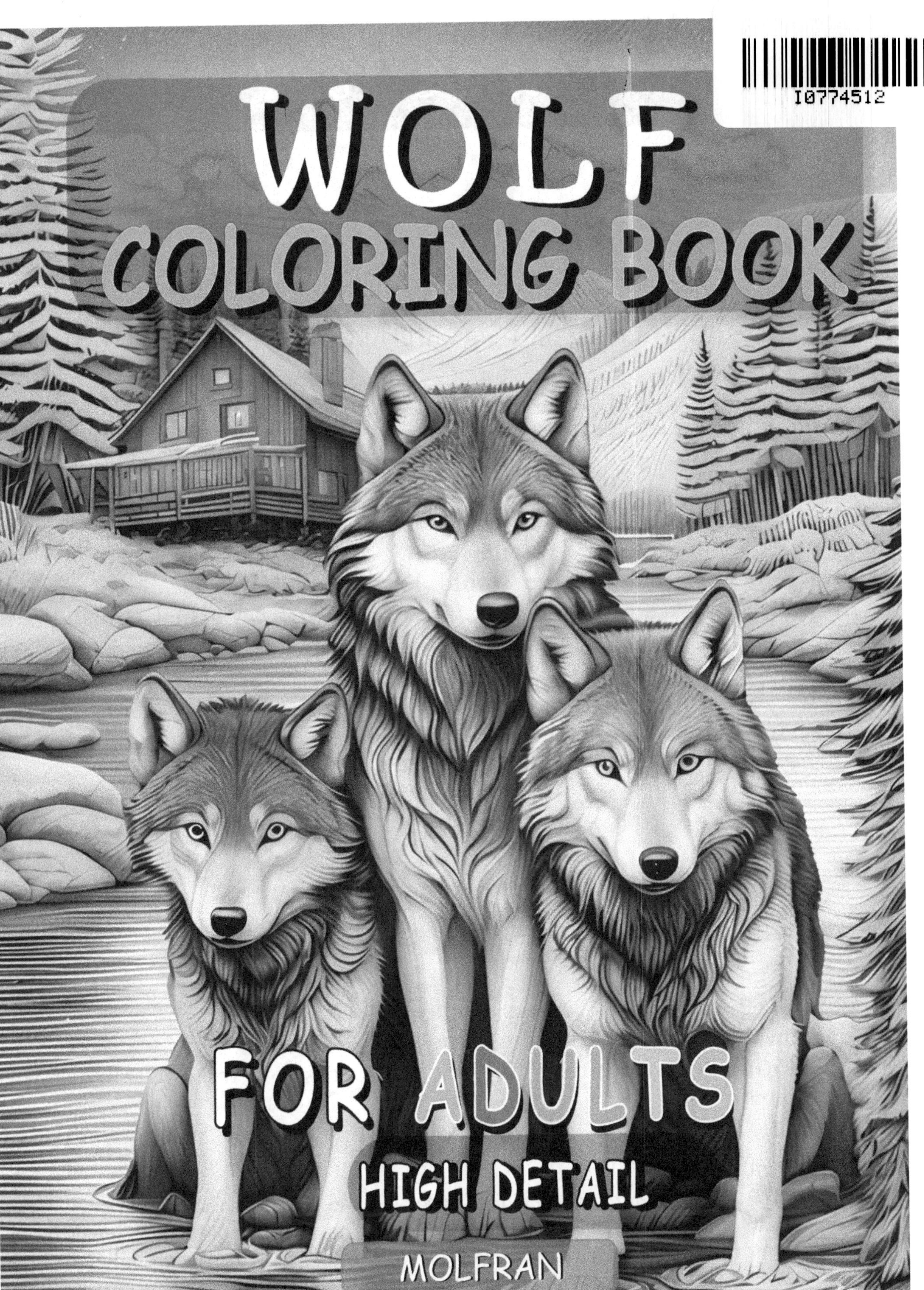

WOLF
COLORING BOOK
FOR ADULTS
HIGH DETAIL
MOLFRAN
I0774512

Thank You!

Dear Reader,

Thank You for Your Purchase!

Congratulations on your new journey with the "Wolf Coloring Book for Adults." Your choice to delve into the intricate world of wolves and artistry is something we deeply value.

We're delighted to express our gratitude by gifting you a beautifully crafted Animal Mandalas Coloring Book for Adults and a playful Cursive Handwriting Workbook for Kids. These gifts are a small gesture of our gratitude and a way to enhance your coloring and learning experience.

We are a new brand and we would love for you to leave us a review on Amazon. Your feedback helps us grow and provides valuable insights to other readers.

To receive your complimentary gifts, simply Scan the QR code below. It's our way of saying thank you for joining our community of coloring enthusiasts.

Once again, thank you for choosing
"Wolf Coloring Book for Adults" We hope it sparks your imagination and fills your world with color.

Happy coloring!

Roy Molina and Cira Franco.

This book belongs to :

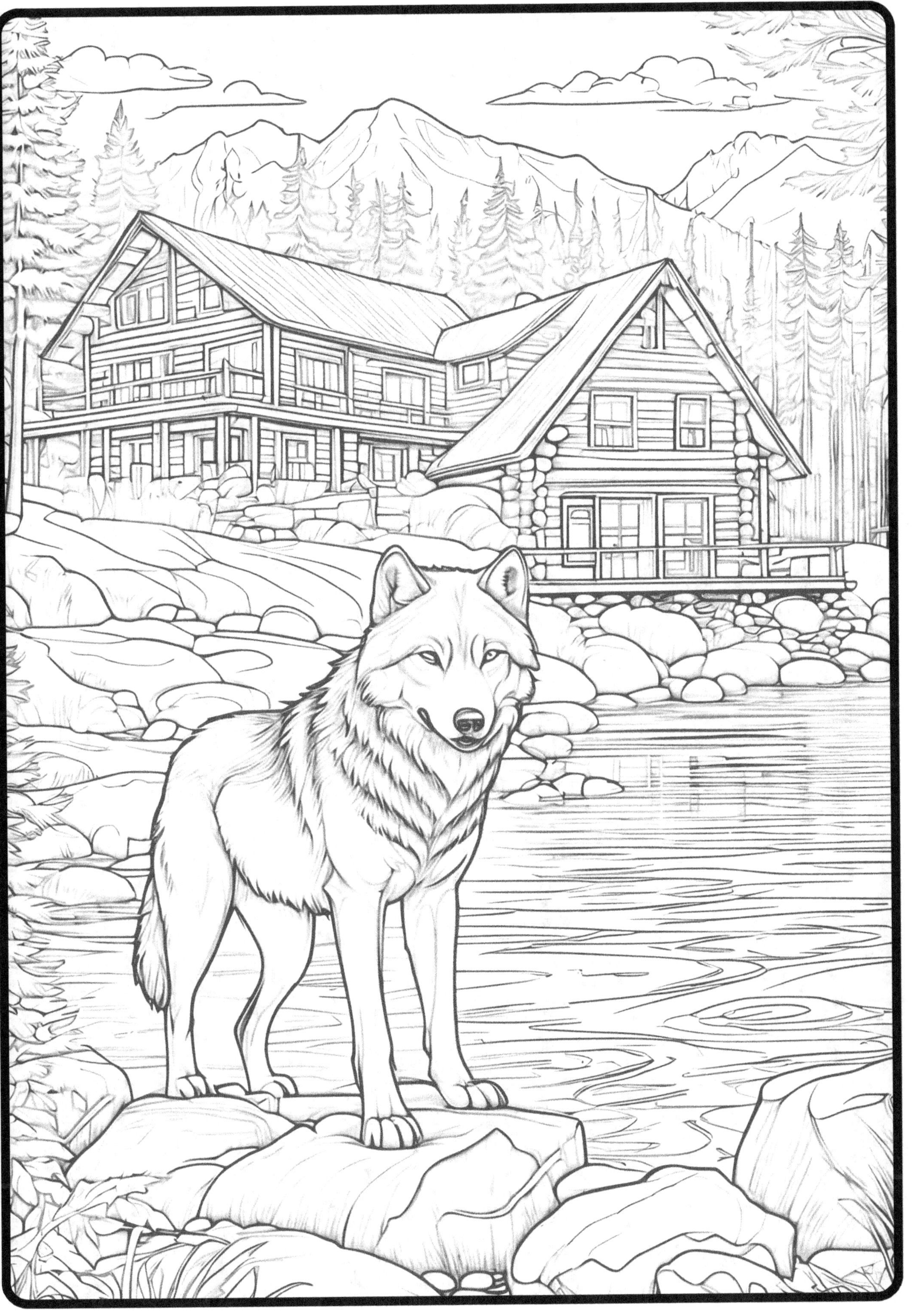

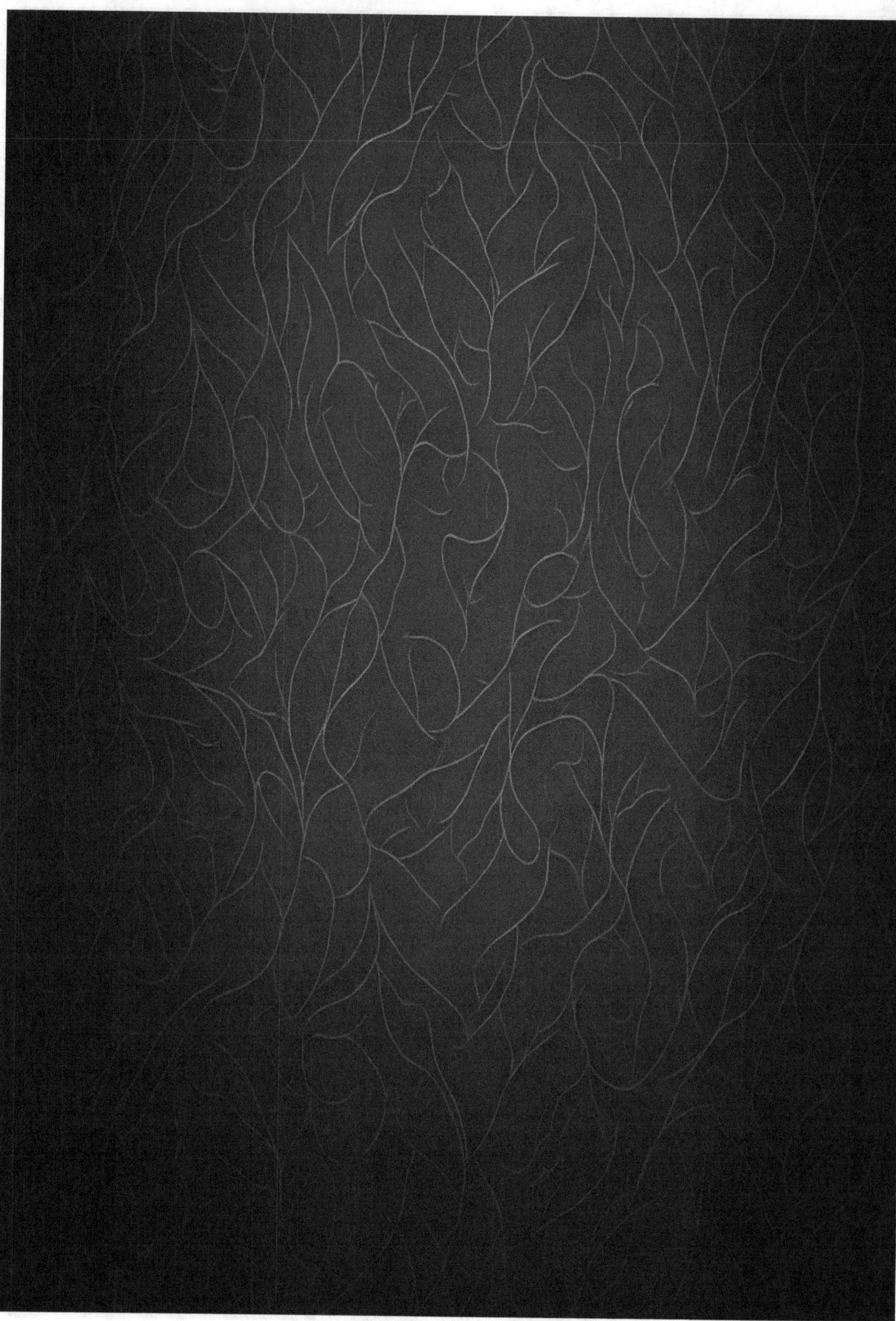

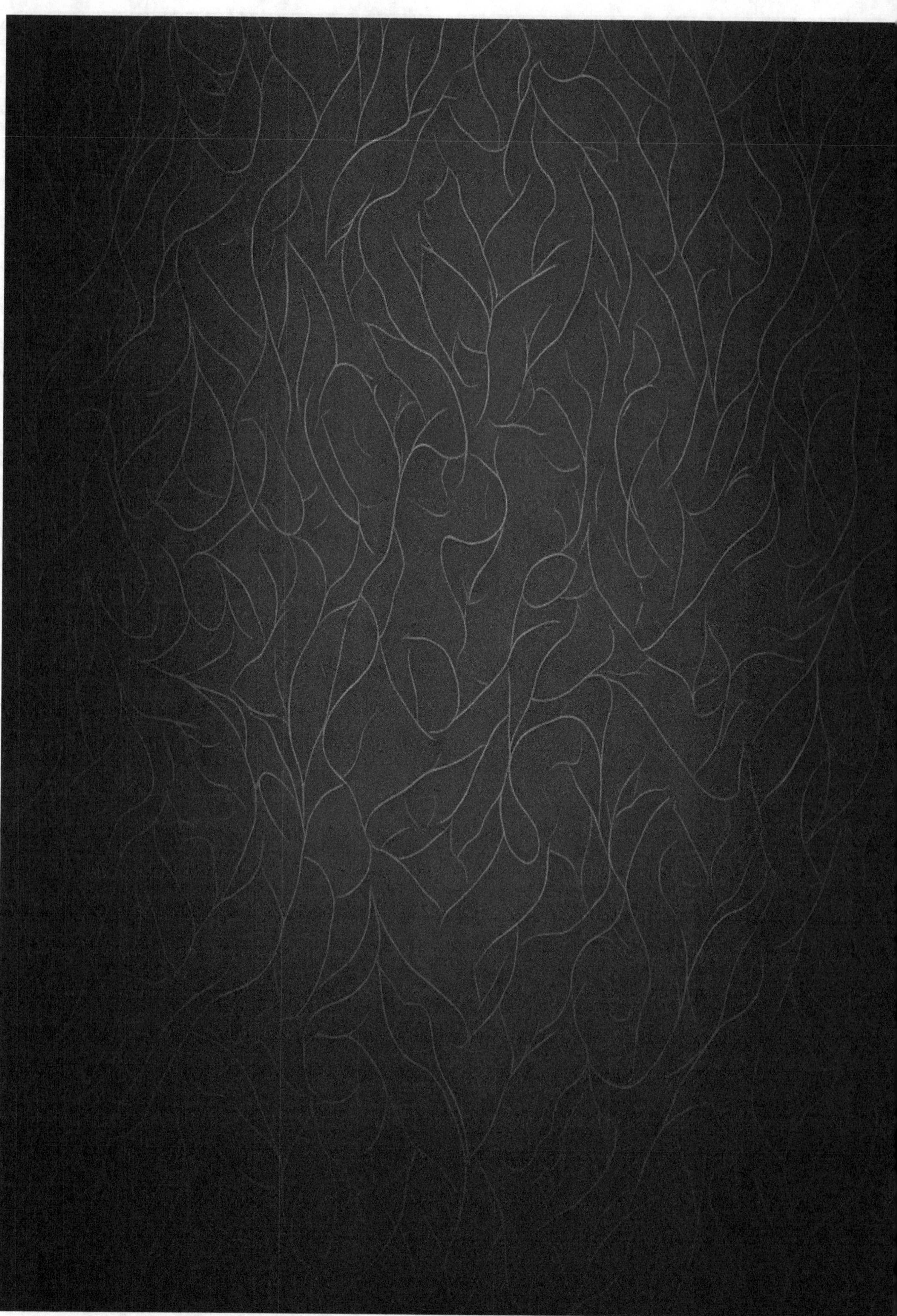

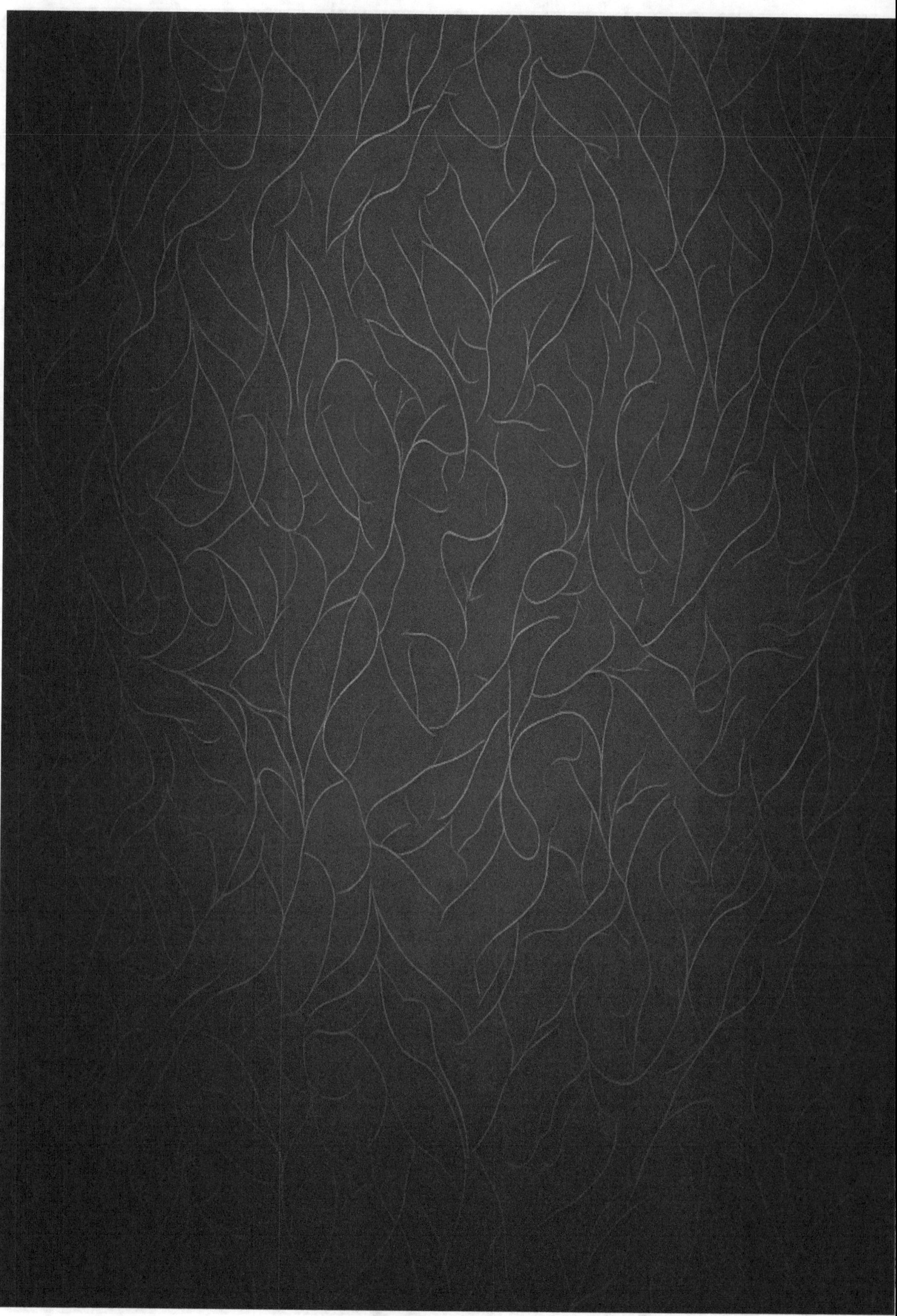

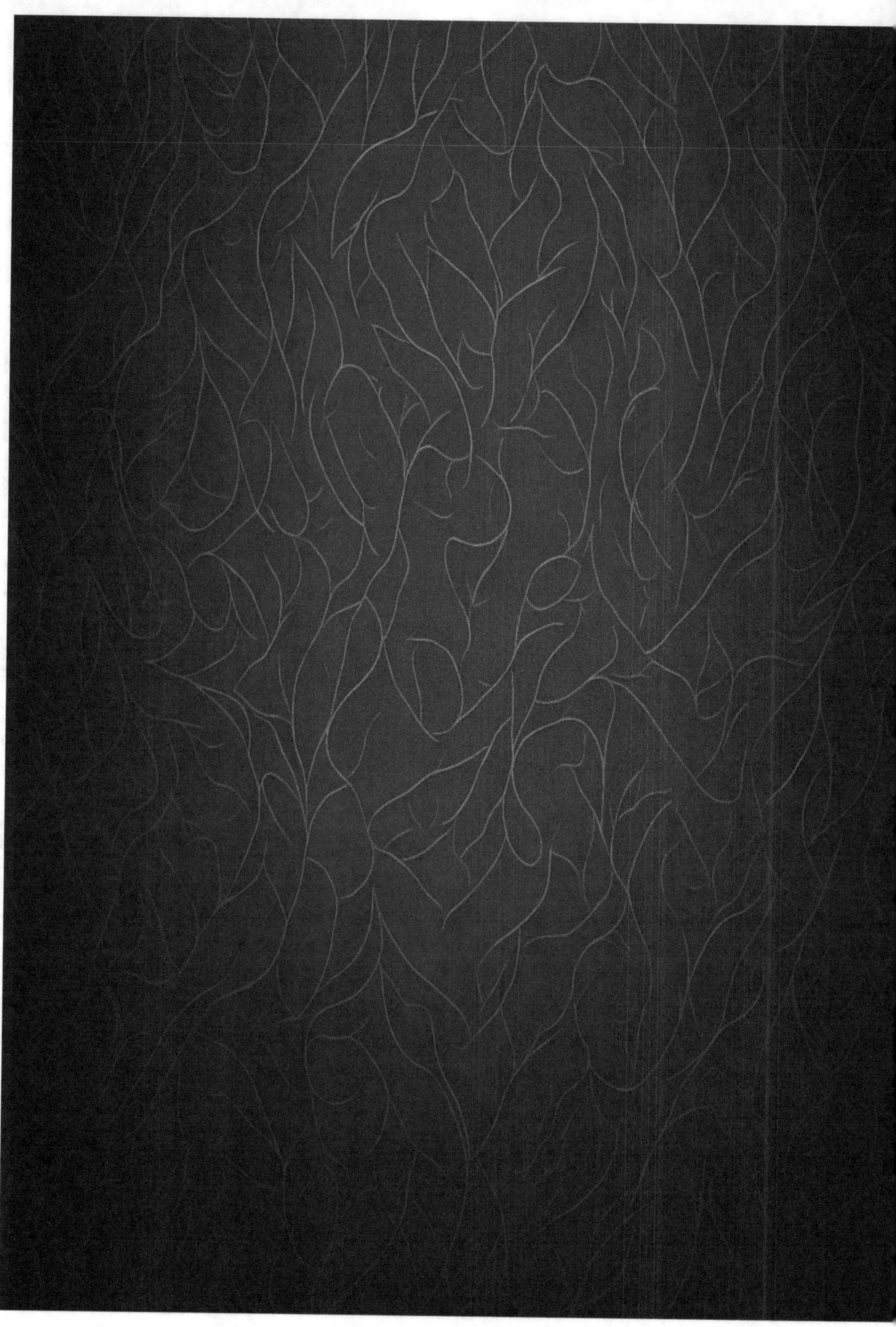

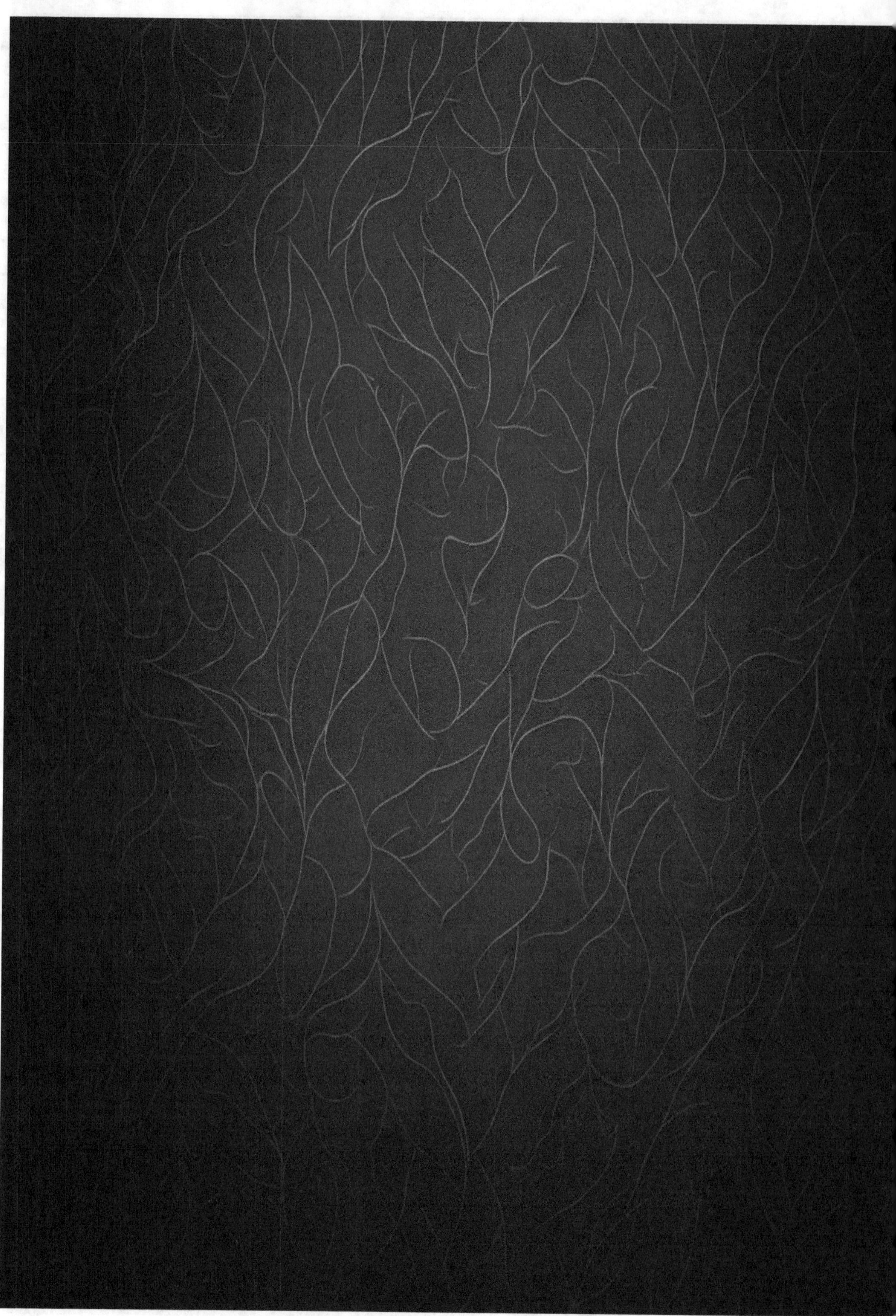

Thank You!

Dear Reader,

Thank You for Your Purchase!

Congratulations on your new journey with the "Wolf Coloring Book for Adults." Your choice to delve into the intricate world of wolves and artistry is something we deeply value.

We're delighted to express our gratitude by gifting you a beautifully crafted Animal Mandalas Coloring Book for Adults and a playful Cursive Handwriting Workbook for Kids. These gifts are a small gesture of our gratitude and a way to enhance your coloring and learning experience.

We are a new brand and we would love for you to leave us a review on Amazon. Your feedback helps us grow and provides valuable insights to other readers.

To receive your complimentary gifts, simply Scan the QR code below. It's our way of saying thank you for joining our community of coloring enthusiasts.

Once again, thank you for choosing "Wolf Coloring Book for Adults" We hope it sparks your imagination and fills your world with color.

Happy coloring!

Roy Molina and Cira Franco.